CHALLENGING THE

BOUNDARIES

OF SLAVERY

David Brion Davis

HARVARD UNIVERSITY PRESS

Cambridge, Massachusetts, and London, England

2003

Printed in the United States of America

Library of Congress Cataloging-in-Publication Data

Davis, David Brion.
Challenging the boundaries of slavery / David Brion Davis.
p. cm. — (The Nathan I. Huggins lectures)
Includes bibliographical references and index.
ISBN 0-674-01182-1 (alk. paper)
1. Slavery—United States—History 2. Antislavery movements—
United States—History. I. Title. II. Series.

E441.D248 2003
306.3'62'0973—dc21   2003041746

For my wonderful daughter-in-law
Alexandra Schimmer

ACKNOWLEDGMENTS

I AM MOST GRATEFUL to Henry Louis Gates Jr. and Harvard's W. E. B. Du Bois Institute and Department of Afro-American Studies for inviting me to give the Nathan I. Huggins Lectures in 2002. Since I had recently had hip surgery and could only deliver the lectures from a wheelchair, my Harvard hosts were especially gracious and helpful in accommodating to this unusual situation. Skip Gates, Anthony Appiah, Werner Sollors, W. Michael Byrd, Linda A. Clayton, Eva L. Maynard, and countless others contributed to my joyful return to the campus where I received my Ph.D. in 1956.

I am much indebted to Stanley L. Engerman, who gave me invaluable criticisms and suggestions, and to John Stauffer, Steven Mintz, and my wife, Toni Hahn Davis, all of whom read and helped me with early drafts. William F. Freehling sent me a timely copy of his lecture "Why Virginia's (Reluctant) Decision to Secede: Menace to Slavery or to State Rights or to ??" which helped to strengthen my thesis on the impact in the South of the British example.

CONTENTS

CHALLENGING THE

BOUNDARIES OF SLAVERY

INTRODUCTION

I HOPE IN THIS SHORT BOOK to present an unconventional experiment in imagining, defining, and challenging certain boundaries related to the history of American slavery. I refer to boundaries in time as well as boundaries in geographic space, in human social and political relations, and in status. For example, a hereditary and absolute monarch or emperor stands above any hierarchies of caste or class, just as a hereditary chattel slave in theory lives below such bounded hierarchies. This could mean that in various past empires a eunuch slave, performing services for a holy emperor, could become an influential intermediary who could cross boundaries like no other person.[1] And as Debra Blumenthal has recently pointed out, while black African slaves in fifteenth-century Valencia were ranked below Moorish, Greek, and Caucasian slaves, they often served as personal armed bodyguards, utilized by their masters to insult or dishonor their masters' enemies or rivals.[2]

With respect to boundaries of time, I have chosen an unorthodox way of being selective. We will move from what I would call macro time to micro time and then move back to a more limited macro period. In other words I will present three ways of viewing the historical place and certain relationships of North American slavery. The first chapter will attempt to provide the "Big Picture," the antecedents and origins of slavery in the New World and then in North America. The second chapter will focus for the most part on a single, seemingly uneventful year, 1819, a year when Frederick Douglass (who never knew his year of birth) turned one and when Herman Melville, Walt Whitman, and Alexander Crummell, the black colonizationist, were born. With the benefit of hindsight, I think we can now see in 1819 the convergence of many trends and symbolic events as well as a foretaste of what American slaveholders and abolitionists would be up against. In the third chapter, moving on from 1819, I will discuss the African-American impact on American abolitionism and then present a thesis regarding the slaveholding South's response to British and French abolitionism and the supposedly disastrous consequences of anti-slavery provocation in the Caribbean. Since the South essentially dominated the federal government from the time of Washington to the time of Lincoln, one must somehow explain the overreaction of Southern leaders to the feeble white and black abolitionist movement in the North. It was their fixation on the Caribbean, I will argue, that led Southerners to escalate their demands, even crossing the boundary of states' rights with the Fugitive Slave Act of 1850, until neutral and moderate Northerners began to fear a true nationalization of the now "peculiar institution."

If the relationship between master and slave exemplified extreme boundaries of power and dehumanization, New World slavery represented a departure from all historical precedents when regions dominated by slave-labor production became separated from such "free soil" polities as England, France, and eventually America's Northern and Northwestern states. For a time the "free soil" regions exploited and even provided African slaves to the colonies or regions that prospered from slave labor, successfully limiting the spread of slavery into their own heartlands. But eventually England took the lead in attempting to impose its own ideals of master-servant "free labor" upon its plantation colonies, and in America many Northerners became alarmed and determined to resist when Southerners challenged all the traditional compromises that had set legal and geographic boundaries to the existence of slavery in the United States.

1

THE ORIGINS AND NATURE
OF NEW WORLD SLAVERY

THE INSTITUTION of chattel slavery is older than
the first human written records, and it has extended
geographically from the medieval Koreans to Pacific
Northwest Indians, from the Aztecs and the far more
primitive Tupinambá of Brazil to the pre-Norman
English and the Norse and Vikings, and to hundreds
of ethnic groups, such as the Ashanti, Mende, Da-
homeans, Igbo, and Tuareg in Africa.

Though we are rightly horrified by the plantation
form of slavery, in which many slaves became cogs in
a highly rationalized system geared for maximum
economic production, we must guard against the
danger of romanticizing pre-modern, largely non-
economic systems of slavery. Such slaves were sometimes subject to cannibalism and ritual sacrifice; they
were always vulnerable to sexual exploitation, tor-
ture, or simply arbitrary death at the whim of an

owner. Because the slave was defined essentially as "not one of us," a captive alien, he or she was always at risk of "bestialization," a word that refers to the degradation and dehumanization signified by the repeated descriptions through history of slaves being stripped naked, driven like cattle, and sold like livestock.[1]

All forms of slavery embody a profound and inherent contradiction, illustrating the most extreme form of a tension we experience almost daily in more subtle or benign interactions of inequality. I refer to the desire to dominate another person until she or he becomes a willing extension of our own will, an instrument to serve our needs. Ideally, for the master or mistress, a slave is a person who has internalized a consuming desire to please and flatter the owner, like a loving pet. Thus in the New Testament Paul tells Titus: "Tell slaves to be submissive to their masters and to give satisfaction in every respect; they are not to talk back, not to pilfer, but to show complete and perfect fidelity." Peter instructs slaves to "accept the authority of your masters with all deference, not only those who are kind and gentle but also those who are harsh." Ideally, from the master's perspective, there should be no boundary separating him from his human tool or instrument. Yet no matter how degraded or responsive to a master's sticks and carrots, the slave is of course an independent center of consciousness, a unique human mind often aware of an owner's weaknesses and capable of defiance, retaliation, or subtle triumphs that uncloak a master's pretensions to godhood.

Since slaves were typically though not always recruited from foreign peoples—and for ancient Greeks the ideal slave was a "barbarian," who spoke a different language—enslavement became an important by-product of intercontinental empires. When we look at examples of great imperial expansion, like that of Rome from the mid-200s B.C.E. to the early Common Era, we find an immense flow of slaves from outlying zones of conquest to Sicily and southern Italy, where slaves transformed the nature of agricultural production on latifundia, or plantations, providing incidentally a crucial precedent in law and practice for the later New World. Many educated American Southerners learned something about the treatment and management of slaves from reading Cato the Elder or Columella's *De re rustica,* works that dealt with discipline as well as positive incentives.

While a few sub-Saharan black slaves mixed with other slaves in the ancient world, the Arabs and their Muslim converts were the first people to make use of millions of blacks from sub-Saharan Africa and to begin associating black Africans with the lowliest forms of bondage. This is not to say that Arabs ever limited bondage to people of sub-Saharan ancestry or practiced the kind of racial oppression that later appeared in white South Africa and most of the New World. Yet any inquiry into the origins of New World slavery must take account of a massive slave revolt that began in 869 in the Common Era and was crushed only in 883 in the marshlands of the Tigris-Euphrates delta, in modern Iraq. The thousands of slaves were blacks, called *Zanj* by the Arabs, and many had originally been transported by sea from East Africa. Worked in regimented gangs, they had been draining and reclaiming wasteland for cultivation— probably of sugarcane and cotton. Though the *Zanj* revolt must be understood within an Islamic social and political context, the Arabs and their Muslim allies were the first people to develop a specialized, long-distance slave trade from sub-Saharan Africa.[2] This fact widens the geographic boundaries for a full understanding of racial slavery in the New World.

Like Judaism and Christianity, Islam emerged at a time when chattel slavery was as universally accepted as human warfare. All three religions sought to regulate and ameliorate slavery. The Hebrew Bible, in

Deuteronomy, even demands giving shelter to and not returning escaped slaves belonging to foreign masters. The prophet Jeremiah condemns ancient Israelites who had reenslaved fellow Jewish slaves after first freeing them. Yet in Leviticus 25:43–46 God tells Moses that since the Hebrews should not sell their own brethren or rule over them "ruthlessly," they should buy their slaves "from the nations round about you":

> You may also buy them from among the
> children of aliens resident among you, or from
> their families that are among you, whom they
> begot in your land. These shall become your
> property: you may keep them as a possession for
> your children after you, for them to inherit as
> property for all time. Such you may treat as
> slaves. But as for your Israelite kinsmen, no one
> shall rule ruthlessly over the other.

The Hebrew Bible or Old Testament thus drew a crucial distinction or boundary between the limited servitude of Jews and the lifelong, hereditary slavery of certain gentiles.

Islam was most explicit in its conviction that freedom, not hereditary slavery, is the natural and presumed status of humankind. And yet Islamic law also gave religious sanction to the enslavement of infidels and to holding even Islamic converts as inheritable slaves, a perpetual status unless a master chose to manumit a particular slave.

The spectacular Arab conquests, like those of the earlier Romans, revolutionized geographic boundaries and produced an immense flow of slaves for employment as servants, soldiers, members of harems, eunuch chaperons, and bureaucrats. Thanks to such earlier innovations as the North Arabian saddle and camel caravans, Arabs, Berbers, and their converts made deep inroads into sub-Saharan Africa, thus tapping, through purchase or capture, an unprecedented pool of slave labor. According to some scholarship, this importation of black slaves into Islamic lands from Spain to India constituted a continuous, large-scale migration—by caravan and sea over a period of more than twelve centuries, beginning in the 600s—that may have equaled in total numbers all the African slaves transported to the Western Hemisphere. One French scholar, Raymond Mauny, estimates that as many as fourteen million African slaves were exported to Muslim regions.[3]

The absence of large populations descended from these millions of African slaves—and there are small communities of blacks in India and the Middle

East—can be explained by the assimilation of blacks over the lapse of many centuries and by the fact that few slave societies have *ever* been capable of natural growth, especially when there has been a large sexual imbalance. Many of the males transported to Muslim lands had been castrated, and there was a much larger demand for females. We should also note that little trace remains today of the large African slave populations in sixteenth- and early seventeenth-century Mexico and Peru. Black slaves once constituted over half the population of both Mexico City and Lima; yet the region that became the United States, which received only about six percent of the slaves shipped to the Americas, contained by 1850 over thirty percent of the African New World Diaspora.

Because the Arab literary sources focus on life in the towns and administrative centers, we know very little about the nature of mining and agricultural labor in the Islamic world, though we do have descriptions of black slaves working in underground mines in Islamic north Africa. It's clear that the explosive expansion of Islam did not lead to capitalist markets and investment, to dramatic economic growth, or to a widespread system of colonial plantation production. Moreover, the Koran and Islamic law, like the earlier Hebrew and Christian Bibles, show no trace or even awareness of what we would term racism. And from the 1500s to the early 1800s, when Moorish corsairs captured European and American ships and raided coastal regions from Italy to Iceland, they showed no compunction about enslaving as many as a million people we would regard as "white."

Yet it's also clear that regardless of their continuing enslavement and purchase of white Christian infidels, medieval Arabs came to associate the most degrading forms of labor with black slaves—with the *Zanj* whom the medieval Arab writer Maqdisi described as "people of black color, flat noses, kinky hair, and little understanding or intelligence." In fact, the Arabic word for slave, *abd,* came in time to mean only a black slave and, in some regions, referred to any black person whether slave or free. Many Arab writers echoed the racial contempt typified by the famous fourteenth-century Tunisian historian Ibn Khaldun when he wrote that black people "are, as a whole submissive to slavery, because Negroes have little that is essentially human and have attributes that are quite similar to those of dumb animals."[4]

There can be no doubt that the increasing purchase or capture of sub-Saharan African slaves for the most degrading kinds of labor generated a form of racism as well as an Islamic literature *defending* the humanity and equality of blacks by explaining the supposed environmental origins of their physical difference. But despite the protests of free black writers themselves, some medieval Muslims continued to describe the *Zanj* as ugly, stupid, dishonest, frivolous and lighthearted, foul-smelling, gifted with a sense of musical rhythm, and dominated by unbridled sexual lust. Point by point, these stereotypes of the medieval Middle East resemble those of the later Spaniards, Portuguese, English, and Americans. While much further research is needed, it seems probable that racial stereotypes were transmitted, along with black slavery itself, from Muslims to Christians and from the eastern Mediterranean to that melting pot of religions and cultures, the Iberian Peninsula.

Meanwhile, northwestern Europe moved gradually from late Roman slavery to serfdom and from serfdom to qualified and what in retrospect have often been overidealized forms of free labor. I cannot begin to summarize here the continuing debates over the reasons for the disappearance of slavery from northwestern Europe by the 1300s or earlier. I will limit myself to two crucial points that involve changing boundaries. First, by the 1500s a nationalism based on an ideal of freedom was developing in countries like England, France, and what would become Holland. Especially during wars, Christians in neighboring countries could be tortured, dismembered, raped, and murdered, but not enslaved in the way that Christians and Muslims had traditionally enslaved one another. Yet these first free-labor nations would much later become the major beneficiaries of the Atlantic Slave System. A kind of Mason-Dixon line would be drawn somewhere in the Atlantic, separating free-labor countries like France, Holland, and England from peripheral colonies based on the slave labor of Indians or especially Africans.

My second point pertains to the persistence and revival of slavery in what had long been Europe's most "progressive" region, the Mediterranean, from the time of the crusades to the colonization of the New World.

As Europe's economy and commerce began to expand in the tenth and eleventh centuries, the first colonies were established not to the West but in the Holy Land. In the 1090s, the First Crusade led to the founding of the Kingdom of Jerusalem, with close commercial ties with Genoa, Pisa, and later Venice. By then Normans had already "liberated" Sicily from the Muslims, enslaving many of the enemy in the process. By the 1100s, various Crusader states had been established at the eastern end of the Mediterranean, and Cyprus had become a base of Venetian power. According to the Belgian historian of medieval slavery, Charles Verlinden, these prototypes of New World colonization required slave labor, especially when they gravitated toward the production of sugar, an extremely labor-intensive crop which would later provide the golden key for New World colonization. There is still some debate and uncertainty over the status of agricultural sugar workers in the Mediterranean, but clearly many slaves were shipped to Cyprus, Crete, and Sicily.[5]

Though some Arab sugar had been imported into Venice in the 900s, the taste of sugar was virtually unknown to Europeans until Crusaders discovered the wondrous sensation of sweetness in Palestine and quickly appropriated Arab sugar fields. Sugarcane had first been domesticated in New Guinea and had very slowly spread to India and the Middle East. Despite the westward spread of sugar cultivation in the Mediterranean, the sweet substance long remained a rare luxury, often used as a medication, available only to the nobility and wealthiest merchants. But then, beginning in the late seventeenth century, the Atlantic Slave System finally transformed the cherished product into the first consumer nutrient for a mass market. Until then, Europeans had had only honey and fruits to supplement dreary, monotonous diets with a shortage of calories. The anthropologist Sydney Mintz has even suggested that the extra calories provided by sugar-sweetened drinks, cakes, and various kinds of confections, together with the need for money to satisfy this new desire for sweetness, contributed to a more disciplined labor force in early industrial Britain.[6] The addiction to sugar's sweetness was accompanied by a more powerful and lethal addiction to a another popular luxury, tobacco, that also was mostly produced by slave labor.

While it is true that tobacco was cultivated for many decades by white indentured servants, long experience in the New World showed that it was almost impossible to induce truly free laborers to work unending shifts in the cane fields and endure the heat and hazards of boiling houses and sugar mills. As the technology was perfected, especially with the invention of three vertical rollers for the crushing of sugarcane, sugar production became in Brazil and then the Caribbean an industrial enterprise—one of the first in human history—requiring heavy capital investment, a large work force of both skilled and unskilled labor, iron-like discipline and supervision, and above all precise timing and the deadlines of an assembly line to transform the perishable cane into finely grained sugar as well as molasses and rum.[7]

Moving back again to origins, Venetian and Genoese merchants were at the forefront in developing conquered Arab sugar-producing regions in the Mediterranean, in supplying slaves for a variety of economic needs in addition to sugar production, and finally in extending the system for slave-grown sugar to the so-called Atlantic islands of Madeira, the Canaries, the Cape Verdes, and São Tomé, off the west coast of Africa. Here I will glance briefly at the changing *sources* of slave labor from the 1100s to the late 1400s, a subject that highlights shifting boundaries and provides perspective on the ultimate choice of Africans.

The Italian merchants had no scruples about selling thousands of Christian slaves to the Muslims of Egypt and Syria. At first they victimized the Slavic inhabitants of the Dalmatian coast, whose ethnic designation in Latin, *sclavus* = Slav, became the origin of the word for slave in English and other Western European languages: *esclave* in French; *esclavo* in Spanish; *sklave* in German. It's notable that the Hebrew, Greek, and Latin words for slave carried no ethnic connotations *(ebed, doulos, servus)*. At first, Slavic captives had been transported across Germany and France to Muslim Spain. But following the Western capture of Constantinople in 1204 in the Fourth Crusade, the Italians established slave trading posts along the northern coast of the Black Sea and the Sea of Azov, much as later European merchants would do along the western coast of Africa. The Genoese and Venetians purchased captive Armenians, Circassians, Georgians, Mingrelians, Russians, Tatars, and Bulgarians—slaves who were no more a distinct people than the so-called Negroes who later ended up as New World slaves. The "Slav" slaves were highly prized in Egypt, Syria, Cyprus, Sicily, eastern Spain, and other Mediterranean markets. They were used for the production of sugar as well as for numerous other tasks. What needs to be stressed is that the Tatars and other slave traders north of the Black Sea were as eager as their later African counterparts to march streams of captives, in this case mostly "white" captives, to coastal markets where they could be exchanged for coveted goods.[8]

Between 1414 and 1423 no fewer than ten thousand slaves, most of them women, were sold in Florence alone. In the early 1400s this white slave trade from the Black Sea foreshadowed almost every aspect of the soon-to-appear African slave trade, from complex organization to permanent posts or forts for trade and long-distance shipment by sea to multinational markets. In fact, while the Portuguese began importing significant numbers of black African slaves in 1444, the region between the Black and Caspian Seas might conceivably have been a source of slaves for New World settlements after 1492.

But in 1453 the Ottoman Turks captured Constantinople and soon diverted the flow of Black Sea and Balkan captives to Islamic markets. Turkish expansion brought an end to Italian colonization efforts in the eastern Mediterranean and sharply reduced Europe's supply of sugar. The Turks also cut off Christian Europe from its major source of slaves, and for most potential buyers the price of slaves became prohibitive. The only alternative to the Crimea and the steppes of western Asia was sub-Saharan Africa, though at the outset far fewer captives were available. For a time, this new demand stimulated the Arab caravan trade across the Sahara, so the black slaves were taken to the shores of Libya and Tunisia and dispersed to Sicily, Naples, Majorca, southern France, and Mediterranean Spain. At the same time, Genoese capital and technology had strengthened Portuguese sea power, and Portugal's harbors had proved to be ideal for the small Italian merchant ships carrying commodities from the Middle East to England and Western Europe. Some of the same Italian merchant and banking families long involved in the Black Sea slave trade now sent agents to Seville and Lisbon where they became pioneers in developing the African slave trade. For example, Bartolomeo Marchionni, who represented one such family, moved in 1470 from Florence to Lisbon. He soon owned sugar plantations in Madeira, worked by black slaves, and the king of Portugal granted him a monopoly for slave trading on the Guinea coast.[9]

Though the Portuguese naval expeditions to West Africa in the mid-1400s were mainly intended to acquire wheat, outflank the Arabs, and find the rich sources of gold and pepper south of Mali, Prince Henry's voyagers also initiated a direct slave trade between West Africa and Lisbon and began to colonize the uninhabited Madeira Islands, at first using as slaves the light-skinned Guanche natives of the Canary Islands.

By the time of Columbus's first American voyage, in 1492, Madeira had already become a wealthy sugar colony mainly dependent on the labor of black African slaves. As the first true colony committed to sugar monoculture and increasingly to black slave labor, Madeira was the transitional prototype for later mercantilist ideals of empire. Madeira soon outstripped the entire Mediterranean in the production of sugar, which Portugal exported by the late 1490s to England, France, Italy, and even the eastern Mediterranean. Columbus, who had lived for more than ten years in Madeira, had the foresight to take sugarcane from the Spanish Canary Islands on his second voyage to the "Indies" in 1493.

Meanwhile, as early as 1495 São Tomé, situated much farther south in the Gulf of Guinea, on the equator, was shipping sugar directly to Antwerp, which would long be the major refining and distributing center for Europe. For the next half-century São Tomé would import more African slaves than Europe, the Americas, or the other Atlantic islands combined. Some wealthy Africans in Angola actually invested in sugar plantations on São Tomé, which also became a gathering place for slaves whom the Portuguese would sell to Africans in exchange for gold on the Gold Coast or, later, ship westward to the Americas. In summary, then, while African slaves were not part of any original European blueprint for colonizing the Americas, spatial boundaries had shifted by the 1490s in a way that would enable Europeans to draw on an enormous potential supply of

African slave labor—aided, I should add, by the favorable system of Atlantic winds and currents, and by the cultivation in Africa of such highly edible New World crops as manioc, which greatly increased the West African population.[10]

We've now surveyed a number of preconditions that would shape and influence New World slavery. There was a tradition extending back to ancient Rome and Greece of reconciling slavery with reason and universal law, and of linking bondage with the expansion of empire. Islamic societies had provided both technical means and moral justifications for exploiting the tribal divisions and ethnic fragmentation of sub-Saharan Africa, a region in which those who opposed exporting slaves, such as the sixteenth-century kings of Jolof, Benin, and Kongo, had few political resources to counteract what the historian Philip Curtin has called "the economics of theft." That is to say, there were few states strong enough to prevent opportunistic African kings, warlords, and merchants from profiting from the low cost of capturing, transporting, and minimally sustaining a captive who could be sold for highly desired commodities—as opposed to the much higher cost of a family's raising, feeding, and training a worker who might be able to produce ivory, textiles, coconuts, or some other goods desired by foreigners. Added to this potential source of slaves who were accustomed to tropical climates and to agricultural work, an incipient racism had emerged in regions where black Africans were known only or primarily as drudge slaves. Since black Africans were seen doing the most degrading and dirty tasks, the false but all-too-human syllogism led to the conclusion that they had been *created* precisely for such work. Finally, the westward drift of sugar cultivation presented the ideal crop for New World development at a time when Western Europe was about to develop internal markets for such other luxury products as eastern spices, tea, coffee, chocolate, and tobacco.

Yet preconditions do not determine the path of historical development. The whole story of New World colonization is haphazard, irrational, and episodic—especially as the Mediterranean patterns of piracy, banditry, plunder, cruelty, and ruthless reprisals were transferred to the Caribbean. In Central America, for example, where the conquistadors were disappointed by the cheapness of tribute in comparison with Mexico, they found some compensation by branding Amerindian slaves on the face and shipping some fifty thousand to Panama, Peru, and the Caribbean.[11] The Portuguese in Brazil relied on Indian slave labor to produce sugar for about a half-century, beginning in the 1530s and 1540s. But it became apparent that African slaves were for cultural reasons far better and more productive workers, in part because most West Africans were accustomed to disciplined and productive labor, while Indians regarded any kind of agriculture as work fit only for women. Indians were also far more susceptible to Old World diseases. Hence Brazilian planters increasingly turned to African slaves, whose purchase price, though much higher than that of Indians, could be equaled by the profits from less than two years of hard labor.[12]

In spite of cultural factors, one could well imagine that Indian slaves, who in the early 1700s made up one-third of the slave labor force in South Carolina, might have become major producers of Caribbean sugar. But in 1500 no one could have predicted the disastrous and appalling effect on Indians of what are called virgin soil epidemics. Of course in the 1300s Europe had suffered from plagues of Asian origin that led to famine in many regions and reduced the total population by at least one-third (in some regions, by fifty percent). A century later, when the Portuguese began exploring the coast of tropical Africa, they suffered mortality rates as high as fifty percent within a few months. Lacking immunity to yellow fever, malaria, and other diseases endemic to tropical Africa, European traders, sailors, soldiers, and missionaries died in incredible numbers until quinine and other prophylactics began to reduce mortality in the mid-nineteenth century. Even the crews of slave ships, having usually spent months at harbors or ports along the African coast, suffered a higher *rate* of mortality than did the slaves themselves on the trans-Atlantic voyage. This point explains why Europeans spent as little time as possible on the West African coast and could hardly have participated in capturing many slaves even if the well-armed African states had permitted them to do so.[13]

But in actuality, it was the Indian populations of the New World that suffered the most catastrophic losses from disease supplemented by Spanish cruelty. Pre-Columbian America had been isolated from the microbial infections that had swept through Asia, Europe, and much of Africa. The New World environment was thus "virgin soil" for pandemics of smallpox, influenza, measles, and other contagious diseases. This virgin-soil disease environment suggests that few if any Europeans or Africans had had significant contact with Native Americans before

1492. The Taino Indians on Hispaniola, the first Spanish New World colony, were virtually exterminated by disease, mass murder, and oppressive labor. Estimates of the island's pre-Columbian population range from a few hundred thousand to several million; by the 1540s there were fewer than five hundred survivors. In Central Mexico a population of perhaps fifteen million in 1519 fell to about 1.5 million a century later, and Andean South America suffered a similar disaster. It's now generally agreed that within a century of Columbus's first voyage, the indigenous population of mainland North and South America had shrunk by about ninety percent, and the Taino of the Caribbean had become almost extinct.[14]

In view of this catastrophe, the worst known in human history, and in view of the Iberians' largely futile but often sincere efforts to protect and Christianize the surviving Indians, it is clear that the New World could never have been "developed" economically without the importation of an immense labor force from some other continent. After Turkish conquests in the East, Europe could not meet this demand with "Slavic slaves" or even with Western indentured labor, as various experiments would show from sixteenth-century Spain to seventeenth-century England. Europe's population was not expanding dramatically, European nations no longer enslaved Christian prisoners of war, and most of the Europeans who could be induced to sail westward were interested in obtaining gold or productive land and being *freed* from the necessity of work. As Cortés put it, he had not come to Mexico to push a plough. Even with the fabulous tales of Aztec and Inca gold, Spain sent far fewer whites to the New World during the sixteenth century than the roughly two hundred fifty thousand African slaves who were shipped to Europe and the Americas in the same period.

The economic historian David Eltis has argued that if economic forces alone had prevailed, Europeans would have revived white slavery, since it would have been cheaper to transport enslaved vagabonds, criminals, and prisoners of war than to sail to Africa and purchase slaves in such a distant region. But this option was negated by whatever cultural forces had brought a sense of unity and freedom to Christians of Western Europe, thus blocking the possibility of any revival of white slavery.[15]

By 1820, in any event, at least ten million African slaves had arrived in the New World, as opposed to a grand total of two million Europeans. And for centuries these Africans performed the most arduous and exhausting work, clearing forests, digging the soil, planting and harvesting the exportable crops that founded economic systems that prospered in ways that eventually attracted untold millions of free immigrants from Europe. Even the non-slave economies of New England and the Middle Atlantic states grew and flourished largely because they supplied the sugar colonies of the West Indies with grain, fish, lumber, iron tools, shoes, clothes, and other products. And if black slaves provided the basic power that drove the interconnected economies of the entire New World, some of their sacrifice is reflected in the fact that by 1820 the original two million white immigrants had engendered a total white New World population of some twelve million, roughly twice as great as the surviving black population. That is to say, the ten million or more Africans imported into the New World had left a population of only about six million by 1820 (the African slave trade, even when illegal, continued to supply hundreds of thousands of slaves to Brazil until 1851 and to Cuba until 1867). Thus by 1820, according to the best informed guesses, there were twice as many whites as blacks in the New World even though there had been about five black African involuntary immigrants for every European who had arrived. When combined with the untold millions of Native Americans who died of disease or oppression within a century of America's so-called discovery, these changes in demographic boundaries are indeed without parallel.

Although I cannot consider all the salient features of New World slavery here, it's important to say a few words about its specifically racial character. First, after many fumbling experiments with Indian slavery and with white indentured and even penal servitude, slavery became indelibly linked throughout the Western Hemisphere with people of African descent. This meant that the dishonor, humiliation, and bestialization that had universally been associated with chattel slavery now became fused with Negritude. The often comic and always degrading stereotypes of the slave—which appear in Roman depictions of Greek and especially Thracian slaves and even in Russian portrayals of serfs who were ethnically indistinguishable from their masters—now merged with the stereotypes of Africans. This linkage, which lies at the heart of white racism, would have disastrous consequences in nineteenth- and twentieth-century South America as well as in the United States.

Second, for complex reasons I can't begin to discuss

here, Latin Americans and even whites in the Caribbean were far more tolerant of racial intermixture
than were North Americans. It was only in North
America that the extremely arbitrary and artificial
concept of "Negro"—denoting anyone with supposedly visible African ancestry, revealed by hair as well
as skin color—took on the stigma of slave heritage.
And I should note in this connection that even apart
from race, even in twentieth-century Africa, a slave
heritage has usually carried a stigma of debasement
and shame. But now, fairly gradually, somatic or
physical characteristics came to signify a new kind of
social and psychological boundary, really an impervi-
ous, Berlin-like wall.

My third point grows out of the second and ap-
plies mainly to the United States. As Orlando Patterson has shown in his classic comparative studies,
slave societies have varied greatly in the restrictions
they've imposed on manumission. Sometimes the
harshest slave systems, such as the one under the
Roman Empire, have taken a very liberal stance
toward the freeing of meritorious (or aging) slaves.
From the American Revolution to about 1820, surprising numbers of slaves were liberated even in the
United States South as well as North. Yet one of the

truly distinctive features of North American slavery, except for that brief period, was the virtual lack of hope for any change in status. This closing of doors and escape hatches resulted partly from the spectacular long-term increase in the value of slaves, which reflected a growing demand and limited supply. The restrictions on manumission also reflected the mounting pressures of white racism—the conviction, shared by virtually every national leader from Jefferson to Lincoln, that whites and blacks could never permanently coexist as free and equal citizens.

This terrible white consensus brings me to the final point: the profound contradiction of a free society that was made possible by black slave labor. Until the late 1700s, none of the slave societies or societies with slaves spread out around the world had committed themselves to the twin ideals of liberty and equality, grounded in a dream or vision of historical progress. And as I've tried to suggest, it was the larger Atlantic Slave System, including North America's trade with the West Indies and the export of Southern rice, tobacco, indigo, and finally cotton and sugar, that prepared the way for everything America was to become. Thus vital links developed between the profit motive, which led to the dehumanization of African slaves, and a conception of the New World as an environment of liberation, opportunity, and upward mobility.

Racial slavery became an intrinsic and indispensable part of New World settlement from Chile to French Canada—not an accidental or unfortunate shortcoming on the margins of the American experience. From the very beginnings, America was part black, and indebted to the appalling sacrifices of millions of individual black men and women who cleared the forests and tilled the soil. Yet even the ardent opponents of slaveholding could seldom if ever acknowledge this basic fact. To balance the soaring aspirations released by the American Revolution and later by evangelical religion, slavery became the dark underside of the American Dream—the great exception to our pretensions of perfection, the single barrier blocking our way to the millennium, the single manifestation of national sin. The tragic result of this formulation was to identify the so-called Negro—and the historically negative connotations of the word are crucial for an understanding of my point—as the Great American Problem.

The road would be clear, everything would be perfect, if it were not for the Negro's presence. Such assumptions tainted some white and even black abolitionist writing, and lay behind the numerous projects and proposals for deporting or colonizing the black population outside the United States. Hence the victims of the great sin of slavery became, in this ghastly psychological inversion, the embodiment of sin. And for some two hundred years African Americans have struggled against accepting or above all *internalizing* this prescribed identity, this psychological curse.

2

1819: SIGNS OF A NEW ERA

HISTORICAL "TURNING POINTS" and "years of decision" can be somewhat misleading if taken too literally. But in retrospect they can be useful in conveying a sense of almost simultaneous occurrences which may be causally unrelated but which point to patterns of convergence, new meanings, and future developments. In many ways, the years 1819–1820 marked a kind of national rite of passage, as Americans crossed new thresholds of decision that transformed the social and intellectual world of the Revolutionary generation.

By 1820, it's worth noting, nearly half of the nation's white population was under the age of sixteen (in the census of 2000, only twenty-one percent of the total population was under fifteen). In 1820 barely twelve percent of white Americans were over the age of forty-three and thus able perhaps to remember news of the American victory at the Battle of Yorktown, only thirty-seven years earlier (that percentage was smaller than the percentage today of all Americans over sixty-five!). Hence in a country swarming with children and youth, President James Monroe, in his early sixties, made a great impression when decked out in a fading Revolutionary War uniform. This was the beginning of a national obsession to keep memories of the Revolution alive.

This goal was reinforced by the so-called Second War of Independence against Britain from 1812 to 1815. Yet that war also helped to accelerate the birth of a new world of manufacturing and continental expansion. One should also stress that the outcome of that war had been extremely uncertain. With a slight change in military fortune, the United States might have gained Upper Canada or lost the Gulf of Mexico coastline and the Lower Mississippi River, with profound consequences for the future of slavery and later continental expansion. Andrew Jackson emerged as the war's great hero, having defeated Britain's "Invincibles" at the Battle of New Orleans before hearing that a peace treaty had already been signed in Europe. Jackson had earlier crushed the powerful Indian tribes of the Southeast, opening the way for their removal to Oklahoma Territory and for the expansion of slavery and King Cotton into the Gulf states.

In 1817–1818 Jackson launched an unauthorized invasion of Spanish East Florida in order to destroy the camps of hostile Indians and fugitive black slaves. Since Spain at that time faced rebellions and independence movements throughout South America, Jackson had a free hand in shipping Florida's Spanish governor off to Cuba and executing two Englishmen accused of inciting the Indians. But in 1819, which happened to be the year of the bloody and repressive Peterloo Massacre in England, Congress plunged into a stormy debate over Jackson's dictatorial actions. Henry Clay likened the general to Caesar and Napoleon, but the votes in the House vindicated Jackson and revealed his rising political power. Crowds cheered Jackson in Philadelphia when he gave a toast to the memory of Benjamin Franklin. But in Baltimore, a city to which we'll soon return, Jackson learned to his dismay that a Senate committee, following a detailed and thorough investigation, had called for an unqualified censure of his invasion of Florida. Infuriated, Jackson headed for Washington and threatened to "cut the ears off" a member of the committee who was a son-in-law of Thomas

Jefferson. A man of violent temper who had killed one antagonist in a duel and had ordered the execution of a supposedly insubordinate teenage recruit, Jackson according to one story was physically restrained in the Senate chamber. But in view of Jackson's triumphal tour, the Senate decided to table the committee's report.[1]

Far more important, Jackson's invasion of Florida strengthened the hand of John Quincy Adams, the secretary of state who was negotiating a crucial treaty with the Spanish minister to the United States, Luis de Onís. Fearing that the United States might support the rebellious Spanish colonies, Onís not only agreed to cede the Floridas to America but accepted America's claims to western territories extending northwest to the Pacific, as part of the disputed boundaries of the Louisiana Purchase. Two years earlier, in 1817, the United States had admitted Mississippi as a slave state, a step now followed by the admission of Alabama, to say nothing of the recognition of Arkansas as a slaveholding territory. As we shall see in the next chapter, the question of imposing boundaries on the expansion of slavery became the explosive issue that finally triggered the Civil War and led unexpectedly to the emancipation of all American slaves.

This dramatic expansion of slaveholding boundaries in the Old Southwest reminded Northerners that according to the Constitution a sparsely populated Southern state had as many Senators as New York or Massachusetts, and that three-fifths of all slaves were counted for purposes of both congressional representation and presidential electoral votes. These measures were a constant incentive to add new slave states to the Union, particularly to balance the migration of non-slaveholding Northerners to Ohio and well beyond. In 1819 work on New York State's Erie Canal had progressed for two years, indicating that farmers in the entire Great Lakes region would eventually have low-cost access to New York City and the Atlantic.

Such questions of expansion and economic growth acquired a new urgency because 1819 brought on the nation's first financial panic and major recession, leading to mass unemployment and suffering. This economic blow extended from artisans and manual laborers in the Eastern cities to the already depressed tobacco economy in Virginia and other Southern states, as the entire nation encountered the shock waves of a modern business cycle.

This was the context in which the federal government faced the most momentous issue in its history, at least to that point, an issue directly related to national self-definition, to the definition of a "republican" form of government, and to the authority to draw boundaries. The basic issue of this "Missouri Crisis" was whether the federal government could impose any limits regarding slavery when admitting new states to the Union, particularly states carved from the vast territory of the Louisiana Purchase of 1803.[2]

Much earlier, even Jefferson had supported a measure in 1784 that would have ended slavery in all the territories west of the Appalachians, and in 1787 Congress had approved the famous Northwest Ordinance, which seemed to guarantee free states north of the Ohio River and east of the Mississippi. Yet in Illinois, admitted as a supposedly free state in 1818, proslavery forces came close to legalizing slavery in an embittered struggle in 1823-1824. Though most political leaders seemed to accept the right of Congress to ban the import of additional slaves from Africa and even to define the Atlantic slave trade as piracy, providing the death penalty for offenders, most Southerners were shocked in February 1819 when a New York congressman, James Tallmadge, proposed to amend a bill that would admit Missouri as a slave state. At that time the territory of Missouri already had about the same number of slaves as New York state, but in 1817 New York had adopted a law that would totally terminate all slavery by 1827.

The Tallmadge Amendment would have prohibited the further introduction of slaves into Missouri, and all children of slaves born in Missouri after its admission as a state would have been freed at age twenty-five. This plan for gradual emancipation was similar to the measures adopted much earlier in five Northern states. In effect, the labor of the slaves' children from age nine or twelve to twenty-five would more than pay the cost of their upbringing, and slaves born before the admission of Missouri would remain slaves for life. But the proposal ignited a prolonged and often violent debate in the House and Senate that dragged on for two years. Some Southerners openly defended slavery as far more just and humane than wage labor in the North and denied that Congress had any power to draw boundaries that excluded such property.

Facing threats of Southern secession and possible civil war, New York's Senator Rufus King, a conservative Federalist who had participated in the Constitutional Convention of 1787 and had continued to call for restrictions on slavery, declared that *any* laws or compacts upholding slavery were "absolutely void, because [they are] contrary to the law of nature, which is the law of God."[3] So far as I know, up to that time no statesman or political leader in the world had publicly made such a radical declaration of slavery's illegality.

The final and famous compromises regarding the Louisiana Purchase allowed for the admission of Missouri as a slave state, with a constitution prohibiting the entry of *free* blacks, and then excluded slavery from the remaining and largely unsettled portions of the Louisiana Purchase north of 36°30′ north latitude, the latitude of Missouri's southern border. Instead of being confined to the original Southeastern states, as many of the nation's Founders had hoped, African-American slavery had thus spread not only westward to the Lower Mississippi Valley but northwestward beyond the Missouri River, backed by a political power that now threatened to make the institution increasingly national.

At this time, in 1819–1820, there were no vigorous or well-organized antislavery groups in either the United States or Britain, though many Northerners were deeply troubled by the admission of Missouri as a new slave state and many Southerners were no less troubled by the new boundary line excluding slavery from most of the Louisiana Purchase.

In the North there was a growing recognition of the failure of the various Northeastern "moral societies" that had sought to preserve communal order and discipline through coercive statutes by appealing to local magistrates and leading citizens. In 1821 a farsighted minister told the Moral Society in Albany, New York, that a free people conscious of their rights could not be coerced by local elites, and that reformers would increasingly need to appeal to public opinion, bypassing local authorities and relying more on what was called "moral influence." This speech was a premonition not only of the temperance and abolition societies that would soon mobilize popular opinion in unprecedented ways but also of the hostile anti-abolitionist mobs that would be incited in the 1830s by local elites or "gentlemen of property and standing."[4]

In 1819 there were many such signs of the quiet and undramatic disappearance of the old provincial Republic. According to an idealized view of this Republic, the artificial limits and distinctions of the Old World had been replaced in America by natural balance, order, simplicity, frugality, and the Jeffersonian hope that a natural aristocracy could succeed in commanding authentic deference from the yeoman-farmer citizenry without the use of patronage or partisan demagoguery. What now seems so striking in retrospect is that actual change appeared to be an orderly continuation of trends from the past, a preservation of the Revolutionary heritage without new revolutionary manifestos or defiant challenges to an old regime.

We have already examined the most portentous change: the westward expansion of King Cotton and of slave states, which, despite the debates over Missouri, led to no antislavery political party but rather to a broad national consensus that the nation's contradictions involving slavery should be repressed or on occasion resolved by compromise. To illustrate other ways that boundaries were expanded and redefined, I will focus on parallels between two classic reinterpretations of classic texts or documents—Chief Justice John Marshall's decision in the Supreme Court case *McCulloch v. Maryland* and William Ellery Channing's "Baltimore Sermon," later entitled "Unitarian Christianity." Both reinterpretations took place in 1819 and both concerned sacred texts: the U.S. Constitution and Holy Scriptures.[5]

By 1819 the Marshall court had established its independence and its right to resolve constitutional conflicts, at least to overturn state laws that conflicted with the federal Constitution. Initially there had been no widely accepted view that the judiciary had a monopoly over constitutional interpretation, and following Jefferson's election in 1800 the Republicans had initiated repeated assaults on both courts and Federalist judges, such as Samuel Chase. But Chief Justice Marshall, appointed in 1801 during John Adams's lame duck presidency, had brilliantly tuned decisions to pressing public needs and had converted the Court, perceived by its enemies as a bastion of outdated Federalist lost causes, into a flexible and pragmatic instrument of capitalistic innovation.

On March 6, 1819, Marshall read the decision of a unanimous Supreme Court in a case involving, among other issues, the critical boundaries of power between American states and nation. According to the traditional Jeffersonian view, the federal union was a creation of the states, and the states remained a barrier of last resort against unconstitutional encroachments by the federal government—dramatized in 1798 by Jefferson's and Madison's Kentucky and Virginia Resolutions. While those attempts to nullify the infamous Alien and Sedition Acts have been hailed as defenses of free speech, the Southern fixation on states' rights was ultimately rooted in a fear of federal or judicial interference with the Southerners' right to define slaves as private property. This fear had been greatly reinforced by Lord Mansfield's famous *Somerset* decision of 1772, which had been interpreted as outlawing slavery in England, and probably by news of similar judicial cases in New England and France, to say nothing of the potentially antislavery actions by some British commanders during the American War of Independence and the War of 1812.

But in 1819 the test on states' rights concerned what anti-Federalists saw as the establishment by Congress of a privileged and monopolistic corporation, the Bank of the United States. Although Jefferson and Hamilton had sharply debated the constitutionality of such a bank in the 1790s, the question had seemingly been resolved in a pragmatic way. In 1816, as a result of economic pressures unleashed by the War of 1812, most of the Jeffersonian Republicans were prepared to support the reinstitution of a national source of credit, even though the bank would be a private corporation, almost free from government supervision. But in 1818 Maryland succeeded in a state court in winning the right to tax the Baltimore branch of the national bank. By early 1819 the exuberant nationalism of the immediate postwar years was beginning to wane, partly because the

United States was plunging into a financial panic and recession. Moreover, irresponsible management by the Bank contributed to a sudden constriction of credit, resulting in an epidemic of bankruptcies. Despite evidence of deep corruption in the Bank's Baltimore branch, efforts in Congress to revoke the Bank's charter had no chance of success.

On March 3, three days before Marshall's decision, William Pinkney, an eminent Baltimore attorney, appealed to the justices "to save the nation," by which Pinkney meant to save the Bank by denying the right of Maryland to tax the Baltimore branch, and by inference the right of other states to tax out of existence a creation of the federal government. No realist could possibly have expected the Marshall court to rule that Congress had no constitutional power to charter a bank. What made *McCulloch* the climactic and most far-reaching decision of the Marshall court was its line of reasoning regarding the nature of the federal Union and the implied powers delegated to Congress.[6]

In upholding the constitutionality of the Bank and in denying the right of Maryland to tax it, Marshall contended that the Constitution had created a new Union and a new sovereign government, a "government of the people" and not a government representing the states. According to Marshall, the

words of the Constitution had to be broadly and flex-
ibly interpreted. For example, Article I, Section 8 con-
tains a list of specific powers delegated to Congress,
and then concludes by saying that Congress can also
"make all laws which shall be necessary and proper
for carrying into execution" the expressly delegated
powers.

Marshall admitted that "the powers of government are limited, and that its limits are not to be
transcended." He insisted, however, that

> the sound construction of the constitution
> must allow to the national legislature that dis-
> cretion, with respect to the means by which the
> powers it confers are to be carried into execu-
> tion, which will enable that body to perform the
> high duties assigned to it, in the manner most
> beneficial to the people. Let the end be legiti-
> mate, let it be within the scope of the constitu-
> tion, and all means which are appropriate, which
> are plainly adapted to that end, which are not
> prohibited, but consistent with the letter and
> spirit of the constitution, are constitutional.[7]

In other words, the states had no power to block,
retard, or control the operation of constitutional
laws passed by Congress, nor could states prevent

Congress from finding the best means, in a pragmatic sense, to accomplish legitimate ends.

Marshall's broad construction immediately provoked a vehement revival of the states' rights and anti-Federalist arguments that had originally been nurtured in the 1760s and 1770s by the colonists' struggles against parliamentary despotism. Writing anonymously, Judge Spencer Roane of the Virginia Court of Appeals said that only a "deplorable idiot" could fail to see that "there is no earthly difference between an *unlimited* grant of power, and a grant limited in its terms, but accompanied with *unlimited* means of carrying it into execution."[8] But regardless of such continuing dissent, which was increasingly confined to the South, Marshall's principles ultimately prevailed, especially in the much later Reconstruction and Civil Rights eras. In 1819 we at least find a vision of the federal government representing the people, not quasi-independent states, and of the federal government choosing the "necessary and proper" means, even when not specified in the Constitution, for establishing justice, ensuring domestic tranquillity, providing for the common defense, and promoting the general welfare.

When the Reverend William Ellery Channing traveled from Boston to Baltimore in late April 1819, the

Philadelphia *Union* was printing anonymous essays by John Marshall defending the *McCulloch* decision. Even if he was not following the controversy raging in the press, Channing, the leader of the New England Unitarians, was surely aware of Marshall's recent decision. For one thing, Channing was a Harvard classmate and friend of Joseph Story, one of the Justices on Marshall's court, who might well have told Channing about a letter from Marshall dated March 24, 1819, and sent to Boston, describing the impending journalistic attacks on their unanimous decision. Further, immediately after graduating from Harvard, Channing had lived in Richmond as a private tutor and had met Marshall, whom he then called "one of the greatest men in the country... Marshall is a great character. He bids fair to be the first character in the Union."[9]

The purpose of Channing's trip to Baltimore was to help install Jared Sparks, one of his young protégés, recently the editor of the *North American Review* (and later a president of Harvard), in one of the first Unitarian pulpits outside New England. Unitarianism represented a liberal repudiation of the Calvinist beliefs in innate human depravity and predestined saints and sinners. Most Unitarians were former Congregationalists or Presbyterians who rejected the traditional Christian doctrines of a Holy Trinity and of a divine Christ who atoned for human sins by accepting bloody sacrifice. Unitarians had quietly begun to dominate Harvard after 1805 and then to win converts among Boston's merchant elite.

The Baltimore congregation was an advance outpost of New England culture in one of the nation's fastest-growing and most promising cities. The ordination ceremony was attended by a galaxy of New England liberals, reformers, and intellectuals, most of them Harvard graduates and many of them future abolitionists. Channing took the occasion to issue a bold but conciliatory reply to the critics of liberal Christianity; his sermon was a semi-official statement of the Unitarian beliefs and principles of that time.[10]

Orthodox Protestants accused the Unitarians of substituting reason for revelation, recalling the ghost of Thomas Paine and the French Revolution. Like Paine, Channing's sermon of May 5 focused on the meaning of the Holy Scriptures, but in a far more respectful way. One revealing passage deserves to be quoted in full:

> We reason about the Bible precisely as civilians [that is, practitioners of civil law] do about the

constitution under which we live; who, as you
know, are accustomed to limit one provision of
that venerable instrument by others, and to fix
the precise import of its parts by inquiring into
its general spirit, into the intentions of its
authors, and into the prevalent feelings, impres-
sions, and circumstances of the time when it
was framed. Without these principles of interpretation, we frankly acknowledge that we
cannot defend the divine authority of the Scriptures. Deny us this latitude, and we must aban-
don this book to its enemies [that is, people like
Thomas Paine].

There was a certain strategic brilliance in drawing
this parallel between the Bible and the Constitution
in Baltimore, the recent battleground of *McCulloch v.
Maryland*. Like Marshall, Channing was not only
reinterpreting a sacred text but redefining intellectual boundaries and arguing for a flexible view of
necessary and proper means. Marshall, as we've seen,
had been concerned with the boundaries of power
between state and federal governments, and had
concluded that there was a direct, unmediated relationship between the people and their federal government, a government limited by constitutional justice

but sovereign in pursuing constitutional means to promote the people's welfare.

Channing, as a Unitarian, rejected the orthodox boundaries between Father, Son, and Holy Ghost. His single God was limited by universal standards of justice and decency, standards that could be called *constitutional* since Channing found them in the very constitution of being—in human reason and in "the obvious and acknowledged laws of nature." Consequently, Channing could not accept a literal and strict-constructionist view of many biblical passages: "Recollect the declarations of Christ, that he came not to send peace but a sword; that unless we eat his flesh and drink his blood we have no life in us; that we must hate father and mother, and pluck out the right eye; and a vast number of passages equally bold and unlimited."

Such passages, Channing complained, were wholly at odds with what he called our idea of "the moral perfection of God." For Channing, God was not an angry and unpredictable father, who commanded the ancient Israelites to wipe out entire ethnic groups, but a progressive parent. "We believe," he affirmed, "that he has a father's concern for his creatures, a father's desire for their improvement." *Improvement* was the key word, and Channing assured his listeners

that God was always delighted by man's improvement. Indeed, God had sent Jesus as a model man,
as the necessary and proper means for promoting
man's self-improvement. In this view, Jesus was
essentially an example of what man could become,
an inspiration to moral perfectibility, liberating men
from self-imposed limits of sin, fatalism, resignation,
and despair. In Channing's scheme, later fulfilled in a
book-length attack on slavery, the Declaration of
Independence and the Revolutionary experience gave
America a special mission for conquering not only
Nature but also all forms of brutishness and irra-
tionality, for creating the kind of society that en-
tailed a duty to promote one's own and others'
happiness. And this union of America's Revolutionary principles and liberal Christianity provided *the*
basis for moral reform. Significantly, Marshall's and
Channing's models of flexible interpretation prepared the way for later challenges of proslavery read-
ings of both the Bible and the Constitution.

I have also dwelt on Channing and Marshall
because the remarkable convergence of their pro-
nouncements, in 1819, presents a microcosm of the
world to come, at least in states north of Baltimore.
Channing stood at the very fountainhead of New
England reform—of a century-long effort to elevate

the tastes, manners, and morals of the nation; to dif-
fuse a culture that was thought to ennoble; to bring
hope and self-respect to the underprivileged by
transmitting the virtues of industry, frugality, temperance, ambition, and self-culture; and above all, to
transform the combative acquisitive, self-indulgent,
and cannibalistic impulses of America into a conscious will for community and brotherhood. In
short, a formula for moral influence that answered
the earlier concerns of the Albany Moral Society.

Although the Unitarians would remain a small
and culturally elitist sect, the major Protestant denominations would gravitate toward Channing's
humanitarian and reformist criteria for interpreting
God's law. This is the way the American Enlighten-
ment merged with evangelical Protestantism. And
while Channing himself delayed speaking out force-
fully on the critical issue of slavery until 1836, he was
the main and acknowledged inspiration for an entire
generation of New England reformers, abolitionists,
and Transcendentalists. Of perhaps even greater sig-
nificance, in 1819 his gentle and rationalistic humani-
tarianism represented what we might label the far
left of American Christianity. In America, orthodox
Protestantism was never challenged by a serious anti-
clerical movement, as it was in Europe. Accordingly,

except for a number of immigrant and ethnic churches in the North, and the Southern churches that increasingly isolated themselves and became embattled over the defense of slavery, American Protestantism never locked itself in a defensive position. Within a relatively short time the major denominations could accept Channing's stress on secular benevolence and the principle, which he announced in 1819, "that all virtue has its foundation in the moral nature of man, that is, in conscience, or his sense of duty, and in the power of forming his temper and life according to conscience."[11]

Channing's sermon, in short, epitomized one of the ways in which nineteenth-century American culture dealt with boundaries—a solution that ultimately came down to the shaping and reformation of individual character, to a faith in the internalization of Christian ideals aided by a God who was as remote but still as earnest and concerned as a Harvard College president. Marshall's decision in *McCulloch,* buttressed by other decisions that I won't mention here, symbolized the other side of an emerging capitalist and modernizing culture. I have only been able to hint at the fact that this broad redefinition of constitutional limits opened new paths for economic aspiration and for the growth of corporate enterprise within a market economy. Suffice it to say that whereas Channing was primarily concerned with individual moral improvement, Marshall was concerned with economic development and with what were then beginning to be called "internal improvements." Marshall's letter to Justice Story of March 24, 1819, which transmitted news about *McCulloch,* was prompted by a friend in Virginia who owned a nail factory and who sought information on a nail-making machine in or near Boston. Marshall's views of congressional power were governed by an entrepreneurial spirit of expediency and compromise that would encourage federal support for roads, canals, railroads, or any other undertakings that promised to stimulate national growth.

In 1819 Channing and Marshall represented two prongs of a common modernizing culture that at once promoted capitalist enterprise and helped to justify it morally and ideologically. The justification came by discrediting the restraints of a premodern religious worldview and by offering moral reforms as an antidote to the disintegration of community. The modernizing culture also stressed the perfectibility of individual character, which placed the ultimate burden of adjustment on the individual.

Of course Marshall and Channing had only dimly

sensed the forces that would begin to transform American society in the 1820s—a decade of rapid economic recovery and growth as well as urbanization in the North accompanied by a major shift from agricultural to nonagricultural employment. As Alexis de Tocqueville acutely saw in 1831, it was the illusion of limitless possibility, of unbounded expectation, that led Americans "continually to change their track for fear of missing the shortest cut to happiness."

In 1819, and long afterwards, there were competing cultures and ideologies in America that struggled to defend traditional limits and boundaries. In the Eastern cities, for example, communities of artisans and mechanics formed one such group. The idealized paternalism of master craftsmen overseeing the training of apprentices and skilled journeymen was as much a part of the old fixed Republican order as were horse-breeders and supposedly paternalistic slaveholders. Later on, Roman Catholic immigrants formed another competing culture. But it was the slaveholding South, already expanding rapidly into the rich cotton lands of Alabama, Mississippi, and Louisiana, that became the major bastion of resistance against Yankee enterprise and Yankee moralism. Nothing would ultimately generate more fear and determined resistance in the South than what these two documents of 1819 symbolized: John Marshall's vision of a powerful federal government, immune from state laws or regulations, coupled with a Constitution so open to flexible and liberal interpretation that it might be turned against slavery itself; and (perhaps even more threatening, though Channing would never condone William Lloyd Garrison's vituperative attacks on the sins of slaveholders) Channing's religious mentality that would convert the Bible into an engine of reform that could be catastrophic for slaveholders. Southerners would especially fear movements for so-called moral improvement that would bypass local elites and mobilize possible mobs of fanatical abolitionists who might bring irresistible pressure on a Marshall-like central government. As we shall see in the next chapter, Great Britain would soon offer Southern leaders a precise scenario of such a nightmare.

3

AFRICAN-AMERICAN ABOLITIONISM AND SOUTHERN FEARS

I WOULD LIKE TO RETURN to one more incident in 1819, my micro year, before tracing certain connections between the macro subject of Anglo-American abolitionism, led in crucial ways by African Americans, and the increasingly paranoid fears of Southern slaveholders. Southern leaders, despite their political success in dominating the nation's federal government and in cultivating much support and economic dependence in Great Britain, their primary customer for cotton, became increasingly obsessed with the dangerous consequences of antislavery agitation. Such consequences, in their eyes, were manifested in the Caribbean from the Haitian Revolution to the economic collapse of the British West Indies following slave emancipation. It was this set of convictions, I shall later argue, that led the South's so-called Slave

Power to take an extremely militant stance that ultimately led to its own destruction.

One place to begin this story is in Philadelphia, where on November 16, 1819, a large number of free African Americans assembled to consider an appeal from the American Colonization Society (ACS) which urged the free people of color in Philadelphia and New York City to give serious thought to the option of emigrating to Africa at the ACS's expense. Black Philadelphians had expressed unease and hostility toward such proposals even before the founding of the white ACS in December 1816. Though they were beginning to be defined, as I suggested in Chapter 1, as the Great American Problem, most free blacks expressed pride in their American heritage and identity. Many had fought or had fathers who had fought in the War of Independence and then the War of 1812. Black leaders were well aware that their people's labor had been essential in creating the nation.

The 1819 meeting, like a more decisive gathering in 1817, was presided over by the wealthy black sailmaker and Revolutionary War veteran James Forten, now aided by the also elite black printer, Russell Parrott. Although in previous years Forten had privately shown much interest in the idea of voluntary colonization, he now saw the ACS, which was led by such famous Southerners as Bushrod Washington (the first president's nephew), Henry Clay, and Andrew Jackson, as an instrument for strengthening slavery by ridding the nation of free blacks, especially successful and educated ones who might provide a model for slaves yearning for freedom. Those who attended the 1819 African-American meeting assured the ACS that "there is but one sentiment among the respectable inhabitants of color . . . which is, that it [emigration] meets their unanimous and decided disapprobation."[1]

The connections between the American antislavery movement and the idea of colonization were extraordinarily complex and have seldom been explained with sufficient clarity by historians. For example, James Forten and a few other elite black leaders in Philadelphia found it necessary to conceal for some years their own support for an African-American colony in Africa. But then they lost faith in the ACS and also recognized that their positions of leadership would be seriously endangered by disagreement with the rank-and-file majority, who had rejected the thought of colonization from the beginning.

The linkage of opposition to slavery with the requirement that freed blacks be returned to Africa appears in some of the earliest and most radical antislavery literature. Thus in 1715 the Quaker John Hepburn appended to his own abolitionist tract an anonymous article, "Arguments Against Making Slaves of Men," which anticipated and answered virtually every proslavery argument that would appear during the next century and a half. Yet this seemingly radical author contended that before being emancipated, all blacks should be given a Christian education and then be returned to Africa, where they could further the causes of religion and civilization. Slaves would have to choose, according to this author, between this form of liberation with free transportation and remaining in bondage in America. The author was well aware of the countless white Christians who had been enslaved by Moors or Turks, Christians who now labored in Islamic lands while longing to be redeemed and returned to Europe. So there were very strong precedents for the idea of an emancipating return.[2]

This formula made more sense when a vast majority of American slaves had been uprooted from their African homelands and could think of an alternative to the racism and oppression in America. In 1773 a group of Massachusetts slaves petitioned the legislature, appealing not only for their natural right to liberty but for an opportunity to "procure money to transport ourselves to some part of the Coast of *Africa,* where we propose a settlement." Early white abolitionists, such as Samuel Hopkins, a bold and radical evangelical minister in the slave-trading town of Newport, Rhode Island, knew that many of the slaves he wished to liberate desired above all to return to Africa. And after the British established the colony of Sierra Leone in 1787 as a refuge for blacks freed during the American War of Independence, it became a supposed haven for many thousands of other blacks crammed into illegal slave ships and then liberated by the British navy. Unfortunately, the heavy mortality and other problems in Sierra Leone hardly made it a utopia.

That said, the example of Sierra Leone also points to less virtuous motives. The large numbers of emancipated slaves taken to Britain after the American Revolution were not welcome in a white nation that had tried to deport all blacks in the late sixteenth century. Even France tried to bar the entry of all blacks in 1777, and in 1778 attempted to outlaw interracial marriages. For the most part, the liberated African Americans in England soon became unemployable paupers and beggars in the street. While Britain's racism was mild by American standards, it is significant that many white prostitutes were in effect deported to Sierra Leone along with the unwanted black refugees from the United States. Seen from one perspective, colonization can be rooted in virulent prejudice and epitomized by the examples of Britain and Russia sending convicts to the Chesapeake, Australia, or Siberia.[3] But from another perspective we can think of humanitarian efforts to rescue Jews and other oppressed groups from an environment of pogroms and potential genocide.

Since the American colonization movement appealed like a political party for maximum public support, including people with quite different and even opposing motives, we need to draw a crucial distinction with respect to racial prejudice. In the first category were the many whites who could not tolerate the thought of living together with free blacks and whose ultimate fear centered on intermixture or what was termed "amalgamation" and much later "miscegenation," which would supposedly contaminate or even wipe out the Anglo-Saxon or white race. The power of such prejudice can be seen in colonial laws that not only banned racial intermarriage but required any slaveholder who manumitted a slave to remove the freedperson from a colony like Virginia within a specified period of time. Later on, such states as Missouri, Indiana, Iowa, and Oregon simply barred the entry of free African Americans. In fact, in our micro year of 1819 even Pennsylvania's House of Representatives received a petition expressing alarm over the increasing number of blacks, including fugitive slaves, who seemed to be pouring into Philadelphia.[4]

This extreme antipathy could be combined with a defense of slavery, as the only condition suitable for such supposedly inferior beings; or it could be connected with a desire to "cleanse" the nation of all blacks, whether slave or free. As I suggested earlier, this kind of impenetrable racial boundary helped to affirm that blacks themselves were the cause of America's promethean contradiction.

The second category includes whites and even blacks who recognized but deplored and hated the depth and near universality of such anti-black prejudice. Since such prejudice seemed certain to persist for many generations, these reformers concluded that voluntary emigration presented the only hope for the children and grandchildren of freed slaves. Nearly all of the leading white abolitionists of the 1830s had earlier supported the ACS or some other form of emigration, typified by Benjamin Lundy's interest in Mexico and Haiti as promising refuges. Even extreme radicals like Gerrit Smith, who acquired

closer ties with blacks than any other white abolitionist except John Brown (whom Smith later supported), long felt that abolitionism could never be
effective in America unless linked in some way with
voluntary colonization.[5]

One must remember that for British and French
abolitionists, the slaves they wished to free were
already "colonized" and there was no major domestic
issue of a biracial society or of freed slaves reducing
the wages of white workers. Since many of the early
Northern leaders of the ACS were sincere abolitionists, there were good reasons why representatives
from the Deep South were the ones who finally, in
the 1820s, killed any prospects for the federal funding
that would have been essential for colonization. In
the eyes of South Carolinians, especially, the ACS was
a Trojan Horse designed to undermine and slowly
destroy slavery, despite its leaders' crafty care in limiting their *official* objectives. The British abolitionists,
Southern leaders kept reminding one another, had
long claimed that their only goal was to outlaw the
African slave trade.

However much we deplore the racism of many colonizationists, we cannot deny that their vision of the
future was more realistic than that of the later abolitionists. W.E.B. Du Bois is often quoted as having

predicted that "the color line" would be the domi-
nant theme of American life in the twentieth century.
But in 1883, twenty years after Lincoln's Emancipation Proclamation, the former slave Frederick
Douglass told a large assemblage of black leaders in
Louisville, Kentucky: "In all relations of life and
death we are met by the color line . . . It hunts us at
midnight, it denies us accommodation . . . excludes
our children from schools . . . compels us to pursue
only such labor as will bring the least reward." Douglass also referred to the "atmosphere of color hate"
that pervaded "churches, courts, and schools, and
worse, the deepest 'sentiment' of ordinary people."[6]

Such thoughts were surely not foreign to Paul
Cuffe, the much earlier wealthy black ship owner
who in many ways was America's pioneer colonizationist. After making contact with British abolitionists in London's African Institution and with local
rulers in Sierra Leone, Cuffe transported thirty-eight
black emigrants from America to Sierra Leone in
1815–1816. Though Cuffe died before he could become
involved in any plans for a mass exodus, he did
become close to both James Forten and the white
clergymen who first organized the ACS. Ministers
like Robert Finley were as interested in Christianiz-
ing Africa and ending the slave trade as in providing

new opportunities for American blacks. Still, they sought to put forces in motion that would abolish American slavery. James Forten initially supported Cuffe's venture, and according to Robert Finley, Forten talked about American blacks remaining a permanently degraded class because "neither riches nor education could put them on a level with the whites, and the more wealthy and better informed any of them became, the more wretched they became."[7]

While Forten would help to lead the campaign against the ACS from August 1817 onward, some of the nation's most prominent and well-educated blacks, including John B. Russwurm, Lott Cary, and Edward W. Blyden, broke ranks and migrated to Liberia, the colony established in 1822 by the ACS. Moreover, many other African Americans moved to Haiti in the 1820s, though most of them returned disillusioned to the United States. Far more blacks, especially fugitive slaves, emigrated to Canada. The notorious Fugitive Slave Law of 1850 conveyed a sense of hopelessness to many African Americans and thus stimulated a new interest in Africa and various proposals for colonization. Nor should one forget the revival of black colonization plans in the post–Civil War era, culminating with Marcus Garvey, who ironically paid warm tribute to the founders of the ACS and who succeeded in the 1920s in mobilizing the first mass movement of African Americans, even if few of his followers were actually prepared to pull up stakes and move to Africa.[8]

Despite these complexities, the crucial and often forgotten point is the way that the Northern free blacks' opposition to slavery and campaign against colonization influenced and shaped the white abolitionist movement of the 1830s and beyond. While James Forten was able to disguise his early support for colonization, he and his elite black colleagues in Philadelphia created the ritual of repudiating and attacking the ACS as proof and symbol of genuine abolitionist commitment some twelve years before William Lloyd Garrison and other whites embraced the same strategy. This new approach, which in Garrison's case led to dishonest misrepresentations and the unscrupulous use of quotations out of context, dismayed many ACS supporters who genuinely wanted to end slavery and who had previously seen proslavery Southerners as their major enemy.[9]

That said, the African-American leadership, beginning with the nameless crowds in Philadelphia who converted Forten, followed by the African-American newspaper *Freedom's Journal* and in 1829 by David

Walker's brilliant *Appeal . . . to the Colored Citizens of the World,* played a crucial part in shaping a Northern antislavery movement that would condemn racial prejudice and demand that freed slaves and whites live together, sharing liberty and legal equality in a post-emancipation America. According to colonizationists of all kinds, these goals were simply unobtainable in what we would call a profoundly racist society. And regardless of the humane intentions of some of the leaders of the ACS, the organization *did* foster racism by picturing blacks as a dangerous people, incapable of being assimilated as equals, even though the ACS also pointed to the glories of ancient Egypt as evidence that American black colonists could build a great Christian civilization in Africa. Any explicit statements of black inferiority by the ACS would have totally undermined the more seriously Christian colonizationists' high expectations for Liberia.

As the historian Julie Winch has recently shown, it was Forten and his fellow black leaders in Philadelphia, including the family of his wealthy and nearly white son-in-law Robert Purvis, who kept radical abolitionism and an opposition to the ACS alive during the 1820s. Aided by the wandering but persistent Quaker abolitionist Benjamin Lundy, they also helped Garrison emerge in the early 1830s as the central figure in American abolitionism. While it was Lundy, a long-time friend of Forten's, who converted Garrison to the cause, it was Garrison's increasing doubts about colonization, evident even when he spoke for an ACS fund-raising event on July 4, 1829, that won him the devotion of James Forten. Forten's continuing flow of monetary contributions kept Garrison's *Liberator* alive, helped Garrison make his fund-raising trip to England, and prepared the way for the creation of the American Anti-Slavery Society in 1833. Forten also played a major part in persuading the extremely wealthy merchant Arthur Tappan to sever his ties with the ACS. In addition to rounding up black subscribers to *The Liberator,* Forten wrote countless letters, some containing highly confidential and negative information on Liberia, which Garrison published in *The Liberator.* Forten's home in Philadelphia also became a stopping place for scores of abolitionists of both races.[10]

In striking contrast to Britain, however, the United States was not a favorable environment for a strong national antislavery movement. Soon after *The Liberator* published a letter from Forten that clearly drew on David Walker's revolutionary *Appeal,* Nat Turner led his famous uprising in Southampton County,

Virginia, killing between fifty-seven and sixty whites, most of them women and children. Both Garrison and Walker, who was already dead, were blamed for inciting this event, and some Southern leaders placed a bounty on Garrison's head and demanded that the governor of Massachusetts suppress *The Liberator*. Congress soon did suppress all antislavery petitions with a so-called Gag Rule, and the Jackson administration intercepted and burned much antislavery mail sent to the South.

From Illinois to Maine abolitionist speakers often faced hostile, stone-throwing crowds, and from Providence to Cincinnati whites led race riots against black inhabitants. As an added barrier, Garrison's vituperative, self-righteous, and venomous style in attacking all slaveholders as egregious sinners offended many potential supporters, including such towering antislavery figures as William Ellery Channing. Moreover, internal bickering and feuding seriously fractured the American abolitionist movement. With respect to the boundaries of reform, British abolitionist leaders from Thomas Clarkson to Thomas Fowell Buxton were not inclined, as the American Garrisonians were, to broaden their mission by embracing feminism, pacifism, and other unpopular causes. Of course these reform movements were based on a vision of human perfectibility and improvement, exemplified by Channing's Baltimore Sermon of 1819. Yet in view of the growing antipathy toward chattel slavery in the Western world, it's noteworthy that prior to the outbreak of the Civil War, American abolitionists failed to achieve a single *national* reform or objective, as distinct from legalizing interracial marriages in Massachusetts and obtaining Personal Liberty laws in some Northern states. But again in contrast to Britain, there was no all-powerful central government that could issue antislavery orders-in-council to so-called crown colonies dependent on slave labor.

As we learn from Don Fehrenbacher's *The Slave-holding Republic,* the American government was increasingly dominated by slaveholders and proslavery interests between the inaugurations of Presidents Washington and Lincoln.[11] Southern slaveholding presidents governed the nation for roughly fifty of those seventy-two years, and four of the six Northern presidents in that span catered to Southern proslavery policies.[12] For example, New York's Millard Fillmore signed the Fugitive Slave Law of 1850, which enforced the return of escaped slaves even from free states, authorized the forcible enlistment of any citizen in the pursuit and capture of fugitives, and endangered every free black person throughout the North.

There were strong economic reasons for the broad national reach of American slavery. Southern slave-grown cotton was by far the nation's leading export. It powered textile-manufacturing revolutions in both New England and England, and it paid for American imports of everything from steel to investment capital. Moreover, since the price of slaves continued to soar through the antebellum decades, American slaves represented more capital than any other asset in the nation, with the exception of land. In 1860 the value of Southern slaves was about three times the value of the capital stock in manufacturing and railroads nationwide. If the U.S. government had made the decision to free all slaves by paying compensation to their owners, the way Britain had done in 1833, the cost would have been both astronomical and unthinkable: the average price of American slaves in 1860 was several times that of British Caribbean slaves in 1833, and there were nearly four million American slaves compared to Britain's nearly eight hundred thousand.

The fortunes of New England manufacturers and New York merchants depended on a northward flow of cotton, a fact that carried the deepest implications

for politics as well as banking, insurance, and shipping. The Southern "lords of the lash" forged ever
closer ties with Northern "lords of the loom." For a
variety of reasons, both economic and political, successful Northern leaders needed to reassure slaveholders that abolitionists like Garrison represented a
lunatic fringe, and that Northerners generally agreed
that the Constitution prevented any interference
with Southern slavery. These were the harsh realities.
And now that we know that slavery was not a back-
ward, inefficient, or unproductive system of labor,
we can see the wisdom in Abraham Lincoln's predic-
tion, in the Lincoln-Douglas debates of 1858, that to
abolish slavery "in the most peaceful way" would
take at least one hundred years.[13] In other words,
anticipating no war, Lincoln was thinking of 1958
and beyond—to the actual years of the Civil Rights
movement.

Yet Southern leaders, especially in the Deep South,
seriously exaggerated the strength of Northern abolitionism and curiously underestimated their own
political strength in the nation. This can partly be
explained by the disunity of the South on a host of
issues apart from the security and perpetuation of
racial slavery. More important was the North's
extraordinary growth and diversification as a result

of massive immigration, urbanization, industrializa-tion, and innovations in transportation. In such a time of momentous changes and uncertainties, some Americans in all sections became fearful of wide-spread conspiracies ranging from the Freemasons to the Money Power and the Catholic Church.

And Southern slaveholders had to face two highly ironic problems: first, Great Britain, the modern world's first "superpower" and by far the largest mar-ket for Southerners' slave-grown cotton, had become by the early 1830s the scene of vast and virtually unopposed petition campaigns and public demon-strations demanding the immediate emancipation of colonial slaves, an objective legally and symbolically achieved in 1833 and genuinely confirmed in 1838. Second, as William Ellery Channing had eloquently insisted, the American slaveholders' founding gener-ation not only had committed the nation to prin-ciples that seemed to clash with all forms of bondage, but had mostly endorsed a consensus that the racial slavery America had inherited was at best a "neces-sary evil" that should in no way be a permanent fix-ture in American life. Yet by the 1820s circumstances had totally changed: it began to appear to many if not most Southerners that their alleged "evil" was far more humane than the new forms of factory labor that had emerged in abolitionist territory, and that political conflicts over such seemingly minor issues as tariffs really involved boundaries of state and federal power that could be matters of life and death.

It is with these thoughts in mind that we should note the remarkable overlapping in time of the famous Nullification crisis, which pitted John C. Calhoun's South Carolina against Andrew Jackson's federal government, on the one hand, and the triumph of abolitionists in Great Britain, on the other. From 1832 to 1833 South Carolina's leaders made it clear that their effort to nullify the federal tariff was a trial run, so to speak, for the defense of slavery from far more insidious intrusions of federal power. The concept of a boundary created by state nullification of a federal law was the very antithesis of John Marshall's *McCulloch v. Maryland.* Yet Carolinians' threats of secession and even civil war became hollow when other Southern states failed to rally against Jackson's assertion of federal power on December 10, 1832. South Carolina's final attempt to save face by nullifying Jackson's "Force Bill" in March 1833 hardly brought any sense of reassurance, especially after Charleston finally received news in late September that the British Parliament had passed its slave emancipation act on August 29, 1833.

Of course the South and especially the Upper South were filled with moderates and unionists of various kinds, and my friend Bill Freehling has reminded me that even slaveholding Virginians did not feel especially threatened by Lincoln's election; indeed, Virginia debated and postponed its decision to secede until April 17, 1861, five days after the bombardment of Fort Sumter, two days after President Lincoln's call for seventy-five thousand volunteers, and five months and ten days after Lincoln's election.

Nearly thirty years earlier, Unionist editorials in South Carolina had accused the secessionists of trying to use news of the British abolitionist movement as a scare tactic to unite slaveholders from other states. Yet Robert J. Turnbull, a low-country planter and writer, had been scrutinizing the British movement for years and conveying a most important message. The British abolitionists, Turnbull emphasized, had begun as a small and seemingly harmless group. William Wilberforce and his followers, for example, had limited their attention to the African slave trade. But then, step by step, Wilberforce and the others had slyly widened their objectives as they mobilized more public support and political power. As early as 1827 Turnbull predicted that this subversive movement would lead to the emancipation of West Indian slaves and then to revolts similar to the Haitian Revolution and total economic ruin in the Caribbean. South Carolina would face the same fate unless the right of Congress even to take a vote on *any* question involving slavery was resisted as "an act of war."[14]

At the heart of much anti-abolitionist writing lay the deep fear of igniting what we might call a "nuclear retribution" on the part of slaves. In the late eighteenth century both English and former French planters repeated the dogma that it had been the publications and agents of the French abolitionists, the Amis des noirs, that had incited the horrors of the Haitian Revolution of 1791–1804, culminating in the self-appointed Emperor Dessalines's order to exterminate all whites remaining on the island. The dogma also held that black slaves were passive, grateful, and obedient unless provoked by subversive whites. Thus public antislavery speeches, such as the 1820 attack on the very legality of bondage by Senator Rufus King, had allegedly played a crucial part in creating the Denmark Vesey conspiracy of 1822. White Baptist missionaries like the Reverend William Knibb were supposedly even more complicit in the great Jamaican slave uprising of 1831, which resulted in only a few white deaths but which by white legend revealed the appalling black Id that slavery suppressed.

Robert M. Harrison, a seasoned diplomat from Virginia who served as America's consul in Jamaica from 1831 to 1858, asked Secretary of State John Forsyth to imagine the feelings of "the friends and relations of those murdered husbands who had their secret parts cut off, and placed in the mouths of their wives and Daughters; and they themselves afterwards violated in the most cruel manner."[15] Similar stories kept the memory of Haiti burning at least at the back of many Southern minds, reconfirming the belief on some level that blacks embodied the very essence of sin. Given the sense of propriety and self-censorship that characterized the Victorian writings of most newspaper editors and diplomats as they responded to British West Indian emancipation, we can only assume that such rumors of the true *ultimate* in dishonor spread as rapidly as did the rumors among Caribbean slaves that a king or European government had already freed them, but that their masters had suppressed the news.

Many influential Southerners were clearly amazed that neither the moment of British emancipation, August 1, 1834, nor the end of so-called apprenticeship, in 1838, was followed by black rebellion, including the rape of many white women. But despite initial British reports of economic and social success,

Southern editors had no difficulty in collecting contrary evidence from Caribbean planters, merchants, and newspapers, often conveyed by the American diplomats in the region, who seem to have been mostly Southerners, and even from British publications like *Blackwood's Magazine* and the London *Times*. The central message was that Negroes were a lazy, indolent people who, because they would not work unless forced to do so, were not qualified for freedom. Ignoring reports from islands like Barbados where there was little marginal land for subsistence agriculture, attention increasingly focused on the large colonies such as Jamaica, Trinidad, and British Guiana, where blacks fled the plantations or worked as little as possible. For Southerners familiar with the writings of such eminent British and French political economists as John R. McCulloch, Edward Gibbon Wakefield, and Jean-Baptiste Say, the total economic failure of West Indian slave emancipation was wholly predictable.[16]

According to Robert Harrison, who had served in the Russian army and was related to President William Henry Harrison, Jamaica faced total ruin by the end of January 1839. By the end of the next year the island's production had supposedly fallen by two-thirds. Secretary of State Abel P. Upshur read the long analysis of a French planter who reported that by 1843 the price of Jamaican freeholds had declined by fifty percent; that a coffee plantation in the parish of St. George, which before emancipation had sold for £7,500, had now been appraised and sold for no more than £1,800. If this economic catastrophe were not bad enough, reports kept flowing out of Jamaica and other colonies of a great increase in Negro crime and conflict between the races. White women, Harrison wrote, were anxiously leaving the island "fearful of worse scenes than took place during the last Insurrection."[17]

For non-economists in England, Thomas Carlyle summed up a growing if still minority consensus in his essay "Occasional Discourse on the Nigger Question," published in 1849. The freed slaves, he wrote, had simply refused to work and the economy of the West Indies had collapsed. Lord Wolseley was convinced that West Indian emancipation had been "a failure in every respect." Anthony Trollope and numerous others conveyed the same message of Negroes "squatting" in idleness, an image confirmed even by a former Chartist, Joseph Barker, who became a strong supporter of the Confederacy after the Civil War began.[18]

Proof of the collapse of British West Indian agriculture could be seen in Britain's frantic search for indentured labor to replace the slaves. In 1840, when some English traders were buying, "freeing," and transporting Africans as indentured servants to the Caribbean, Calhoun bitterly remarked on the British hypocrisy of holding over one hundred million slaves in India, which was nothing but "a huge British plantation." Despite the immense distance from the Caribbean, the British did eventually turn to India as a source of hundreds of thousands of plantation workers for Jamaica, Trinidad, and Guyana. A Southern newspaper quoted from the *New York Journal of Commerce* that on a 131-day voyage from Singapore to Jamaica, 90 of the 261 so-called coolies died. Yet, as Southern leaders happily observed, the British colonies could never catch up with the major beneficiaries of their drastic mistake, Cuba and Brazil, which continued to import and use black slaves for their production of sugar and coffee.[19]

But why would a highly successful imperialist nation like Britain make such a momentous mistake? Duff Green, the influential editor of the *United States Telegraph,* whose daughter married Calhoun's son, advanced a theory that won increasing support in the South and that echoed explanations heard in France and other regions skeptical of British philanthropy.

If the British were truly motivated by philanthropy, Green asked, why did they oppress and starve the Irish? British abolitionism was simply a front or mask for British manufacturers with an East India interest. The capitalists were intent on developing mass markets for their own produce as well as cheaper sources of cotton and other tropical materials in populous India and the East Indies. They also calculated that despite the drop in West India production, freed slaves would consume more British exports. Far more alarming, as numerous Southern leaders maintained, the British were determined to abolish slavery in the United States and elsewhere, especially after discovering how their own policies had undermined their own competitive advantage.[20]

Regardless of the inconsistencies of such arguments, they catered to the strong American Anglophobia that helped to picture Northern abolitionists as the tools or agents of a vast British conspiracy to destroy the world's only great Republic. From the early 1830s to the 1840s a number of crises arose when the British liberated American slaves on coastal ships that sought refuge in Bermuda or Nassau as the result of storms, or, in one case, after a successful slave revolt. These British challenges to American slave law brought threats of war and were reinforced by the arrival in the North of British abolitionists like George Thompson, who was pictured as a secret agent from perfidious Albion, sent "to foment discord among our people, array brother against brother [and] to excite treasonable opposition to our government." Understandably, Thompson's life was soon in peril. Various Southern editors warned that British agents and British gold were being used to incite Southern slaves "to rise and butcher their masters" and bring on a war that would overthrow the republican form of government. In the South there was even much talk of the British using armed former slaves from the Caribbean to invade South Carolina or the Gulf states and ignite a Haiti-like slave revolution. This was the context in which President John Tyler and Secretary of State Calhoun annexed Texas in 1845.[21]

Seven years earlier former President John Quincy Adams, now an antislavery congressman, had argued that the Southern Slave Power had engineered the Texas Revolution of 1836 and the drive for annexing Texas as one or more slave states. Mounting a three-week filibuster, Adams presented hundreds of antislavery petitions and finally defeated a move to annex Texas by joint resolution. But then in 1843 Duff Green, President Tyler's secret agent in Britain and France, informed Tyler's ardently proslavery government that Britain was about to guarantee interest on a loan to Texas on the condition that Texans abolish slavery. The plan would make Texas a British satellite and a place of refuge, like Canada, for fugitive slaves from the United States. Green claimed that, by erecting a barrier of freedom across the southwestern flank of the slaveholding states, the British could effectively join Northern abolitionists in destroying both slavery and the federal Union.

Like many myths, this elaborate fantasy rested on a thin foundation of truth. Britain was eager to keep Texas from reviving the slave trade from Africa, and when Calhoun became secretary of state he could make public the British government's private statement that Britain "desires, and is constantly exerting herself to procure, the general abolition of slavery throughout the world." By skillfully distorting and publicizing the British diplomatic notes, Calhoun tried to identify the anti-annexation cause with a British plot to destroy the Union. He also lectured the British on the blessings of black slavery, employing faulty statistics from the census of 1840 to argue that emancipation in the North had produced black insanity, crime, suicide, and degeneracy. He sternly informed Mexico that because of the British conspiracy to subvert Southern slavery, the United States was forced to annex Texas in self-defense.[22]

The expansionist administrations of Tyler and Polk dramatized the South's overreaction to the alleged abolitionist threat. The result was an escalation of demands, such as the insistence of Calhoun and other South Carolinian leaders that slavery could not be excluded even from Oregon or any other new territory acquired by the United States. Slavery, in short, had to be boundaryless, an ideal reinforced by the increasing Southern interest in buying or seizing Cuba.[23]

Though this extremist drive to open the way for slavery in all territories culminated in the repeal of the Missouri Compromise by the Kansas-Nebraska Act and the Dred Scott decision, slaveholders in the Deep South were still not reassured or satisfied. Manisha Sinha, in her recent book *The Counter-Revolution of Slavery,* documents the surprising importance in South Carolina of the movement to reopen the African slave trade beginning in the early 1850s as well as the desire for independence and the growing hostility toward democracy among low-country planters. The escalating demands for the moral vindication and even nationalization of slavery aroused increasing concern among large numbers of non-abolitionist Northerners who would never have dreamed of interfering with slavery in the existing states of the Old South. For many Northerners who would gravitate to the new Republican party, it did suddenly appear that the nation had long been in the grip of an expansive Slave Power that had achieved a long succession of unmitigated victories until in 1858 Kansas voters rejected the proslavery Lecompton Constitution by a vote of ten to one. Ironically, by continually overreacting to a somewhat neutral, complacent, and racist North, Southern militants created an *antislavery* North in the sense that many Northerners felt personally and justifiably threatened by an undemocratic Slave Power.[24]

This did not mean that Northern white men were prepared to die for the liberation of Southern slaves. Far from it. But when we survey the forces in motion in the late 1850s and early 1860s, nothing is more striking than the fortuity of events. If Virginia and the Upper South had not seceded, would the war have ended quickly and slavery been preserved? If George McClellan had been a better general or Robert E. Lee a less brilliant one, would the Union have won without an emancipation decree? If Southern leaders had been less Anglophobic, would Prime Minister Palmerston have been more open to the arguments of Gladstone, Lord Russell, and Napoleon III, and have intervened in a way to ensure Confederate independence?

However one views such questions, I still believe that it was almost providential that by April 1861 the nation was in the hands of a highly skilled politician who sincerely believed that, as he put it, if slavery was not wrong, nothing was wrong. A man who believed, in terms of boundaries, that the "proposition" of equal rights, upon which the nation had been founded, included "*all*" men," regardless, as he put it, of "color, size, intellect, moral development, or social capacity."[25]

NOTES

INDEX

NOTES

Introduction

1 Orlando Patterson, *Slavery and Social Death: A Comparative Study* (Cambridge, Mass.: Harvard University Press, 1982), 299–333.

2 Debra Blumenthal, "Implements of Labor, Instruments of Honour: Muslim, Eastern and Black African Slaves in Fifteenth-Century Valencia" (Ph.D. dissertation, University of Toronto, 2000); Blumenthal's "Defending Their Masters' Honour: Slaves as Violent Offenders in Fifteenth-Century Valencia," will appear in a volume entitled *Medieval Violence* (Toronto: University of Toronto Press, forthcoming).

1. The Origins and Nature of New World Slavery

1 See my essay "At the Heart of Slavery," in David Brion Davis, *In the Image of God: Religion, Moral Values, and Our Heritage of Slavery* (New Haven: Yale University Press, 2001), 123–136.

2 See the many sources I cite in Davis, *Slavery and Human Progress* (New York: Oxford University Press, 1984), 321–322.

3 Raymond Mauny, *Les siècles obscures de l'Afrique noir: Histoire et archéologie* (Paris, 1990), 240ff; *American Sociological Review,* 62 (December 1997), 921–936.

4 Maqdisi and Ibn Khaldun quoted in Bernard Lewis, *Race and Slavery in the Middle East: An Historical Enquiry* (New York: Oxford University Press, 1990), 52, 53.

5 Charles Verlinden, *L'esclavage dans l'Europe médiévale,* vol. 1: *Péninsule ibérique, France* (Bruge, 1955); vol. 2: *Italie—Colonies italiennes du Levant—Levant latin—Empire byzantin* (Gent, 1977); Verlinden, *The Beginnings of Modern Colonization: Eleven Essays with an Introduction,* trans. Yvonne Freccero (Ithaca, N.Y.: Cornell University Press, 1970).

6 Sidney W. Mintz, *Sweetness and Power: The Place of Sugar in Modern History* (New York: Viking, 1985).

7 See especially Stuart B. Schwartz, *Sugar Plantations in the Formation of Brazilian Society: Bahia, 1550–1835* (Cambridge: Cambridge University Press, 1985).

8 Davis, *Slavery and Human Progress,* 51–82.

9 Ibid.; Hugh Thomas, *The Slave Trade* (New York: Simon and Schuster, 1997), 10–11, 13–14, 84–86.

10 For São Tomé, see especially Schwartz, *Sugar Plantations,* 13–17, and Davis, *Slavery and Human Progress,* 61, 63, 68, 71, 95–96.

11 William L. Sherman, *Forced Native Labor in Sixteenth-Century Central America* (Lincoln: University of Nebraska Press, 1979), 64–82. This enslavement of Central American Indians proceeded despite the preventive efforts of the Spanish Crown. When a Nicaraguan governor ordered that Indian slaves be freed and sent home, the natives, "some of whom were women and suckling children, had their face brands canceled. Fresh letters spelling 'libre' were burned into their scarred faces" (64–65).

12 Schwartz, *Sugar Plantations,* 51–72.

13 For the power of Africans and their rough equality with Europeans in trade negotiations, see John Thornton, *Africa and Africans in the Making of the Atlantic World, 1400–1780* (New York: Cambridge University Press, 1992). Given the lack of reliable statistics, there is inevitable debate over these estimates.

14 Alfred W. Crosby Jr., "Virgin Soil Epidemics as a Factor in the Aboriginal Depopulation of America," *William and Mary Quarterly,* 33 (1976), 289–299; Calvin Martin, *Keepers of the Game: Indian-Animal Relationships and the Fur Trade* (Berkeley: University of California Press, 1978).

15 David Eltis, *The Rise of African Slavery in the Americas* (Cambridge: Cambridge University Press, 2000), 57–84.

2. 1819: Signs of a New Era

1 Robert V. Remini, *Andrew Jackson and the Course of American Empire, 1767–1821* (New York: Harper and Row, 1977), 341–398; Michael Paul Rogin, *Fathers and Children: Andrew Jackson and the Subjugation of the American Indian* (New York: Knopf, 1975), 165–205.

2 The best study of the Missouri crisis that I've read is Robert P. Forbes's Yale doctoral dissertation, "Slavery and the Meaning of America, 1819–1833" (University Microfilm, 1994); the standard though dated work is Glover Moore, *The Missouri Controversy, 1819–1821* (Lexington: University of Kentucky Press, 1953).

3 Robert Ernst, *Rufus King: American Federalist* (Chapel Hill: University of North Carolina Press), 372. Ernst notes that "Senator [William] Smith of South Carolina reported that King said this on Feb. 11 [1820] . . . King's speeches were not reported, but from incomplete drafts and notes, Smith's and Pinkney's rebuttals, and contemporary correspondence, one can infer that King had arrived at new high ground." Ernst then quotes

from a draft of an undated letter in which King expressed the same argument. Douglas R. Egerton, in his work on the controversial Denmark Vesey slave conspiracy of 1822, notes that many blacks in the Senate galleries heard King's speeches and that one of Vesey's co-conspirators in Charleston reported that "Mr. King was the black man's friend"; Egerton, *He Shall Go Out Free: The Lives of Denmark Vesey* (Madison, Wis.: Madison House, 1999), 130–131. Whatever the truth regarding Vesey's conspiracy, King's publicized remarks reinforced white South Carolinians' conviction that abolitionism and public condemnations of slavery could ignite a repetition of the Haitian Revolution in the American South.

4 For the emergence of American reform movements, see Robert H. Abzug, *Cosmos Crumbling: American Reform in the Religious Imagination* (New York: Oxford University Press, 1994), and Steven Mintz, *Moralists and Modernizers: America's Pre–Civil War Reformers* (Baltimore: Johns Hopkins University Press, 1995); for anti-abolitionists, Leonard L. Richards, *"Gentlemen of Property and Standing": Anti-Abolition Mobs in Jacksonian America* (New York: Oxford University Press, 1990). For the example of the Reverend John Chester's address to the Albany Moral Society, I am

indebted to a student paper, written long ago, by Dr. Joel Bernard.

5 For the text of *McCulloch v. Maryland,* see <www.tourolaw.edu/patch/McCulloch>; for Channing's sermon, "Unitarian Christianity," in *The Works of William E. Channing, D.D.* (Boston: American Unitarian Association, 1899), 367–384, available at <www.athens.net/~wells/unitxty.htm>.

6 Also in 1819, the Supreme Court held that the charter of Dartmouth College, granted in 1769 by King George III, was a contract that could not be impaired by the New Hampshire legislature. The decision was far-reaching in its application to business charters, eventually protecting many businesses and corporations from government regulation.

7 <www.tourolaw.edu/patch/McCulloch>.

8 Article from the *Enquirer* reprinted in *John P. Branch Historical Papers of Randolph-Macon College* (June 1905), 80.

9 William Henry Channing, ed., *The Life of William Ellery Channing, D.D.* (1880; Hicksville, N.Y., 1975), 51. In this letter Channing strongly endorsed Marshall's opposition to the Federalist Alien and Sedition laws.

10 Channing, "Unitarian Christianity," 367–384.

11 Ibid., 380.

3. African-American Abolitionism and Southern Fears

1 See Julie Winch, *A Gentleman of Color: The Life of James Forten* (New York: Oxford University Press, 2002), 198–199.

2 John Hepburn, *The American Defence of the Christian Golden Rule, or an Essay to Prove the Unlawfulness of Making Slaves of Men* (1715), 23–43.

3 Though when England stopped sending convicts to Australia in 1840, one of the strongest arguments was the question "What was the punishment in being sent where so many free labourers were anxious to go?" A.G.L. Shaw, *Convicts and the Colonies: A Study of Penal Transportation from Great Britain and Ireland to Australia and Other Parts of the British Empire* (London: Faber and Faber, n.d.), 275.

4 Julie Winch, *Philadelphia's Black Elite: Activism, Accommodation, and the Struggle for Autonomy, 1787–1848* (Philadelphia: Temple University Press, 1988), 20.

5 See especially John Stauffer, *The Black Hearts of Men: Radical Abolitionists and the Transformation of Race* (Cambridge, Mass.: Harvard University Press, 2001), 87–88, 94, 97–105, 265–266.

6 *The Frederick Douglass Papers,* series 1: *Speeches, Debates, and Interviews,* vol. 5: *1881–95,* ed. John W. Blassingame and John R. McKivigan (New Haven: Yale University Press, 1992), 92–96.

7 Winch, *Philadelphia's Black Elite,* 37.

8 *Marcus Garvey and UNIA Papers,* vol. 4 (Berkeley: University of California Press, 1985), 632–633; vol. 5 (Berkeley: University of California Press, 1986), 586–587, 610.

9 My own study of Garrison's misrepresentation of ACS texts confirms the charges made by John L. Thomas in his prize-winning book, *The Liberator: William Lloyd Garrison, A Biography* (Boston: Little, Brown, 1963), 148–149.

10 Winch, *A Gentleman of Color,* passim; Richard S. Newman, *The Transformation of American Abolitionism: Fighting Slavery in the Early Republic* (Chapel Hill: University of North Carolina Press, 2002), 112–116; Henry Mayer, *All on Fire: William Lloyd Garrison and the Abolition of Slavery* (New York: St. Martin's, 1998), 101, 110, 116, 147, 173. While Mayer gives some recognition to Forten's aid and names James G. Barbadoes as Garrison's "chief black ally" in Philadelphia, Winch shows that Forten's support and influence were considerably stronger than previous historians have recognized.

11 Don Fehrenbacher, *The Slaveholding Republic: An Account of the United States Government's Relations with Slavery* (New York: Oxford University Press, 2001).

12 I exempt John and John Quincy Adams, though the latter had worked for certain proslavery inter-

ests when he was secretary of state. John Adams's secret support of Toussaint Louverture, in the Haitian Revolution, was perhaps the strongest antislavery measure taken by a president in this entire period. Of course John Quincy Adams's later defense of the *Amistad* captives before the Supreme Court and his struggle as a congressman against the Gag Rule probably classify him as America's leading antislavery statesman even though he rejected the label of "abolitionist"; see especially Leonard L. Richards, *The Life and Times of Congressman John Quincy Adams* (New York: Oxford University Press, 1986).

13 *Created Equal? The Complete Lincoln-Douglas Debates of 1858,* ed. Paul M. Angle (Chicago: University of Chicago Press, 1958), 270.

14 Joe Bassette Wilkins Jr., "Window on Freedom: The South's Response to the Emancipation of the Slaves in the British West Indies, 1833–1861" (Ph.D. dissertation, University of South Carolina, 1977), 57–62. I have learned much from this excellent, well-researched, and unfortunately neglected work.

15 Harrison to Forsyth, November 14, 1834, quoted ibid., 123.

16 Seymour Drescher, *The Mighty Experiment: Free Labor versus Slavery in British Emancipation* (New

York: Oxford University Press, 2002), 54–72. Drescher demonstrates dramatically that most historians have been egregiously wrong in assuming that political economists following Adam Smith agreed without hesitation on the superiority of free to slave labor. The British abolitionist movement had to ignore or simply defy the consensus of contemporary economists.

17   Wilkins, "Window on Freedom," 107, 114–116, 133, 144–146.

18   R. J. M. Blackett, *Divided Hearts: Britain and the American Civil War* (Baton Rouge: Louisiana State University Press, 2001), 118–119. William Ellery Channing, in a lecture glorifying British West Indian emancipation, insisted that the event was "invested with holiness and moral sublimity." "Address on the Anniversary of Emancipation in the British West Indies," in *The Works of William E. Channing, D.D.* (Boston: American Unitarian Association, 1899), 914.

19   Largely as a result of British pressure, Brazil stopped importing African slaves by 1851, but the slave trade to Cuba continued to 1867. In Britain, antislavery protests put an early stop to the slave-like shipment of "indentured" Africans to the West Indies and delayed the major transportation of Asian workers to replace the slaves.

20 Drescher, *Mighty Experiment,* 44–50; Frederick
    Merk, *Slavery and the Annexation of Texas* (New
    York: Knopf, 1972), 14, 26–31, 187–192, 221–225,
    230–236, 258–264, 275–280; Wilkins, "Window on
    Freedom," 45–49, 99–100, 151.

21 Merk, *Slavery and the Annexation of Texas,* passim;
    Wilkins, "Window on Freedom," passim.

22 Merk, *Slavery and the Annexation of Texas,* 44–151,
    204–212, 217–290; Wilkins, "Window on Freedom,"
    168–214.

23 Manisha Sinha, *The Counter-Revolution of Slavery:
    Politics and Ideology in Antebellum South Carolina*
    (Chapel Hill: University of North Carolina Press,
    2000), 68–69. Frederick Merk, *Manifest Destiny and
    Mission in American History: A Reinterpretation* (New
    York: Knopf, 1963), 209–211.

24 Leonard L. Richards, *The Slave Power: The Free
    North and Southern Domination, 1780–1860* (Baton
    Rouge: Louisiana State University Press, 2000);
    David Brion Davis, *The Slave Power Conspiracy and
    the Paranoid Style* (Baton Rouge: Louisiana State
    University Press, 1969). While in the latter book I
    in no way sought to minimize the reality of "The
    Slave Power" (many readers misinterpreted the
    meaning that Richard Hofstadter and I attached
    to the phrase "paranoid style"), I have come in
    recent years to better appreciate the *degree* to

which Southern slaveholders ruled what Don Fehrenbacher has termed "the Slaveholding Republic." And yet, as I argue here, this "power" in no way reassured Southern leaders, who became increasingly "paranoid" in their view of the anti-slavery menace.

25 Garry Wills, *Lincoln at Gettysburg: The Words That Remade America* (New York: Simon and Schuster, 1992), 100, 105. For other views of Lincoln's understanding of the Declaration of Independence, see William Lee Miller, *Lincoln's Virtues: An Ethical Biography* (New York: Knopf, 2002), 351–353, 372–373; and David Herbert Donald, *Lincoln* (New York: Simon and Schuster, 1995), 176, 201–202, 222, 224, 226.

INDEX

Bahamas, 86

Baltimore, Md., 37, 44, 46–47, 49–52, 54, 75

Bank of the United States, 46–47

Barbadoes, James G., 102n10

Barbados, 83

Barker, Joseph, 84

Belgium, 21

Benin, 22

Berbers, 10

Bermuda, 86

Bible, 6, 9, 12, 44, 51–54, 59

Black Sea, 18–20

Blackwood's Magazine, 83

Blumenthal, Debra, 1

Blyden, Edward W., 70

Boston, Mass., 49–51, 57

Brazil, 5, 16, 23–24, 28, 85, 104n19

Britain, 5, 13–14, 20, 26, 37, 42, 101n3, 104n19; aboli-tionism in, 2, 68, 73–75, 79–81, 86–88; West Indies colonies, 3–4, 61, 76, 80–87, 104n18; and sugar, 16, 21; wars with United States, 36, 46, 65; emanci-

pation in, 46, 79, 82–84, 104n18; and the South, 59, 61, 68, 78–88, 90–91; settlement of Sierra Leone, 65–66, 69

Brown, John, 68

Bulgarians, 18

Buxton, Thomas Fowell, 74

Calhoun, John C., 79, 85, 87–89

Canada, 32, 70, 88

Canary Islands, 17, 20–21

Cape Verde Islands, 17

Capitalism, 45, 56–57, 86, 104n16

Carlyle, Thomas, 84

Cary, Lott, 70

Catholics, 58, 78

Cato the Elder, 7

Channing, William Ellery, 44, 49–57, 59, 74–75, 78, 104n18

Charleston, S.C., 79, 99n3

Chase, Samuel, 45

Chester, John, 99n4

Chile, 32